ENGLISH
MADE SUPER SUPER EASY BOOK 1

LOOK AND LEARN

ACTIVITY BOOK FOR ENGLISH LEARNERS
A MUST FOR ALL BEGINNERS

EVELYN SAMUEL

ENGLISH

Made Super

Super Easy

BOOK 1

First Edition Published by Evelyn Samuel

Copyright © 2023 Evelyn Samuel

Eve Super Easy Books

ISBN: 9781916744004

www.EveSuperEasyBooks.com

evesupereasybooks@gmail.com

All rights reversed. Neither this book, nor any parts within it may be sold or reproduced in any form without permission.

No part of this book may be reproduced in any form or by any

electronic or mechanical means including information storage and retrieval systems, without permission in writing from the author.

The only exception is by a reviewer, who may quote short excerpts in a review.

The purpose of this book is to educate and entertain.

The views and opinions expressed in this book are that of the author based on her personal experiences and education. The author does not guarantee that anyone following the techniques, suggestions, ideas or strategies will become successful.

The author shall neither be liable nor responsible for any loss or damage allegedly arising from any information or suggestion in this book.

PREFACE

English Book1 teaches new learners the basic of the English language. Book 1 introduces the student to simple words. Each word is next to its picture. Simple tasks are used to test recall and use of the word.

FOREWARD

What a **super super easy** way to study and understand the English language. Words in picture form make it easy to recall, understand, and spell.

REVIEWS

★★★★★ **Fantastic book**
Reviewed 24 June 2023
Fun and easy to use.

★★★★★ **Brilliant!**
Reviewed 26 June 2023
I highly recommend this book. The pictures make the words come to life. My spelling and use of the words have improved.

AUTHOR

|  | Evelyn Samuel is an established author and an expert in teaching English language to first time learners. |

A

LOOK AND LEARN

1

ANT	
APE	
ARM	
APPLE	
ARROW	

A

MATCH THE WORD WITH THE PICTURE

ANT	
APE	
ARM	
APPLE	
ARROW	

2

	3
# A	
SPELLING	
ANT	
APE	
ARM	
APPLE	
ARROW	

A

GRAMMAR

This is an ant.

This is an ape.

This is an arm.

This is an apple.

This is an arrow.

A

SENTENCE

I saw an ant.	
I played with an ape.	
I broke my arm.	
I ate an apple.	
I shot an arrow.	

A

PRESENT TENSE	PAST TENSE
See	Saw
Play	Played
Break	Broke
Eat	Ate
Shoot	Shot

B

LOOK AND LEARN

BAT

BALL

BIRD

BUCKET

BULL

B

8

MATCH THE WORD WITH THE PICTURE

BAT

BALL

BIRD

BUCKET

BULL

B

	9
SPELLING	
BAT	
BALL	
BIRD	
BUCKET	
BULL	

B

10

GRAMMAR

This is a bat.	
This is a ball.	
This is a bird.	
This is a bucket.	
This is a bull.	

B

11

SENTENCE

I played with a bat.

I kicked a ball.

I fed a bird.

I carried a bucket.

I ran with a bull.

B

PRESENT TENSE	PAST TENSE
Play	Played
Kick	Kicked
Feed	Fed
Carry	Carried
Run	Ran

C

LOOK AND LEARN

CAT	
CAR	
CUP	
COW	
CAKE	

C

14

MATCH THE WORD WITH THE PICTURE

CAT	
CAR	
CUP	
COW	
CAKE	

C

SPELLING

CAT	
CAR	
CUP	
COW	
CAKE	

15

C

GRAMMAR

This is a cat.

This is a car.

This is a cup.

This is a cow.

This is a cake.

C

SENTENCE

I played with a cat.

I drove a car.

I bought a cup.

I saw a cow.

I ate a cake.

PRESENT TENSE	PAST TENSE
Play	Played
Drive	Drove
Buy	Bought
See	Saw
Eat	Ate

D

LOOK AND LEARN

DOG

DAD

DUCK

DOOR

DEER

D

MATCH THE WORD WITH THE PICTURE

DOG

DAD

DUCK

DOOR

DEER

D

SPELLING

DOG	
DAD	
DUCK	
DOOR	
DEER	

D

GRAMMAR

This is a dog.

This is my dad.

This is a duck.

This is a door.

This is a deer.

D

SENTENCE

I carried a dog.

I love my dad.

I played with a duck

I closed the door.

I saw a deer.

D

PRESENT TENSE	PAST TENSE
Carry	Carried
Love	Loved
Play	Played
Close	Closed
See	Saw

E

LOOK AND LEARN

EGG	
EYE	
EAR	
EAGLE	
ELEPHANT	

E

MATCH THE WORD WITH THE PICTURE

EGG	
EYE	
EAR	
EAGLE	
ELEPHANT	

26

E

	27
SPELLING	
EGG	
EYE	
EAR	
EAGLE	
ELEPHANT	

E

GRAMMAR

This is an egg.

This is an eye.

This is an ear.

This is an eagle.

This is an elephant.

E

29

SENTENCE	
I ate an egg.	
I closed my eye.	
I cleaned my ear.	
I saw an eagle.	
I played with an elephant.	

E

PRESENT TENSE	PAST TENSE
Eat	Ate
Close	Closed
Clean	Cleaned
See	Saw
Play	Played

F

LOOK AND LEARN

31

FOX

FAN

FACE

FARM

FROG

F

MATCH THE WORD WITH THE PICTURE

32

| FOX |
| FAN |
| FACE |
| FARM |
| FROG |

	33
# F	
SPELLING	
FOX	
FAN	
FACE	
FARM	
Frog	

F

34

GRAMMAR

This is a fox.

This is a fan.

This is a face.

This is a farm.

This is an frog.

F

SENTENCE

I saw a fox.

I bought a fan.

I washed my face.

I live on a farm.

I played with a frog.

F

PRESENT TENSE	PAST TENSE
See	Saw
Wash	Washed
Live	Lived
Play	Played
Buy	Bought

G

LOOK AND LEARN

GIRL	
GATE	
GOAT	
GAME	
GLOVE	

G

MATCH THE WORD WITH THE PICTURE

38

GIRL	
GATE	
GOAT	
GAME	
GLOVE	

G

39

SPELLING	
GIRL	
GATE	
GOAT	
GAME	
GLOVE	

G

40

GRAMMAR

This is a girl.

This is a gate.

This is a goat.

This is a game.

This is a glove.

G

SENTENCE

I met a girl.

I pushed a gate.

I saw a goat.

I played a game.

I wore a glove.

G

PRESENT TENSE	PAST TENSE
Meet	Met
Push	Pushed
See	Saw
Play	Played
Wear	Wore

H

LOOK AND LEARN

HEN

HAT

HAND

HOUSE

HORSE

H

MATCH THE WORD WITH THE PICTURE

44

HEN	
HAT	
HAND	
HOUSE	
HORSE	

H

SPELLING

HEN	
HAT	
HAND	
HOUSE	
HORSE	

H

GRAMMAR

This is a hen.

This is a hat.

This is a hand.

This is a house.

This is a horse.

H

SENTENCE

I played with a hen.

I wore a hat.

I broke my hand.

I cleaned the house.

I rode a horse.

H

PRESENT TENSE	PAST TENSE
Play	Played
wear	Wore
break	Broke
Clean	Cleaned
ride	Rode

I

LOOK AND LEARN

49

ICE	
IRON	
IGLOO	
INSECT	
ISLAND	

I

MATCH THE WORD WITH THE PICTURE

ICE	
IRON	
IGLOO	
INSECT	
ISLAND	

I

SPELLING

ICE	
IRON	
IGLOO	
INSECT	
ISLAND	

I i

GRAMMAR

This is an ice cube.

This is an iron.

This is an igloo.

This is an insect.

This is an island.

I

SENTENCE

I ate an ice cube.

I bought an iron.

I saw an igloo.

I played with an insect.

I visited an Island.

PRESENT TENSE	PAST TENSE
Eat	Ate
Buy	Bought
See	Saw
Play	Played
Visit	Visited

J

LOOK AND LEARN

JAM	
JAIL	
JEWEL	
JACKET	
JACKAL	

J

MATCH THE WORD WITH THE PICTURE

JAM	
JAIL	
JEWEL	
JACKET	
JACKAL	

J

SPELLING

JAM	
JAIL	
JEWEL	
JACKET	
JACKAL	

J

GRAMMAR

This is a jam tart .

This is a jail .

This is a pretty jewel .

This is a jacket.

This is a jackal.

J

SENTENCE

I ate a jam tart.

I visited a jail.

I bought a pretty jewel.

I wore a jacket.

I saw a jackal.

J

PRESENT TENSE	PAST TENSE
Eat	Ate
Visit	Visited
Buy	Bought
See	Saw
Play	Played

K

LOOK AND LEARN

KEY	
KITE	
KITTEN	
KETTLE	
KITCHEN	

K

MATCH THE WORD WITH THE PICTURE

KEY	
KITE	
KITTEN	
KETTLE	
KITCHEN	

K

	63
SPELLING	
KEY	
KITE	
KITTEN	
KETTLE	
KITCHEN	

K

GRAMMAR

This is a key.

This is a kite.

This is a kitten.

This is a kettle.

This is a kitchen.

K

SENTENCE

I lost a key.

I flew a kite.

I played with a kitten.

I bought a kettle.

I cleaned a kitchen.

K

PRESENT TENSE	PAST TENSE
Lose	Lost
Fly	Flew
Play	Played
Buy	Bought
Clean	Cleaned

L

LOOK AND LEARN

LIP	
LEAF	
LAMP	
LADY	
LEMON	

L

68

MATCH THE WORD WITH THE PICTURE

LIP	
LEAF	
LAMP	
LADY	
LEMON	

L

SPELLING

LIP	
LEAF	
LAMP	
LADY	
LEMON	

69

L

GRAMMAR

This is a lip.

This is a leaf.

This is a lamp.

This is a lady.

This is a lemon.

L

SENTENCE

I bit my lip.

I drew a leaf.

I lit a lamp.

I met a lady.

I ate a lemon.

L

PRESENT TENSE	PAST TENSE
Bite	Bit
Draw	Drew
Eat	Ate
Light	Lit
Meet	Met

M

LOOK AND LEARN

MAT	
MAN	
MILK	
MONEY	
MONKEY	

M

MATCH THE WORD WITH THE PICTURE

74

MAT	
MAN	
MILK	
MONEY	
MONKEY	

M

SPELLING

MAT	
MAN	
MILK	
MONEY	
MONKEY	

M

GRAMMAR

This is a mat.

This is a man.

This is milk.

This is money.

This is a monkey.

M

SENTENCE

I sat on a mat.

I met a man.

I drank milk.

I lost money.

I played with a monkey.

M

PRESENT TENSE	PAST TENSE
Sit	Sat
Meet	Met
Drink	Drank
Lose	Lost
Play	Played

N

LOOK AND LEARN

79

NET	
NECK	
NOSE	
NAIL	
NURSE	

N

80

MATCH THE WORD WITH THE PICTURE

NET	
NECK	
NOSE	
NAIL	
NURSE	

N

	81
SPELLING	
NET	
NECK	
NOSE	
NAIL	
NURSE	

N

82

GRAMMAR

This is a net.

This is a neck.

This is a nose.

This is a nail.

This is a nurse.

N

SENTENCE

I have a net.

I hurt my neck.

I blew my nose.

I broke a nail.

I met a nurse.

N

PRESENT TENSE	PAST TENSE
Have	Had
Hurt	Hurt
Blow	Blew
Brake	Broke
Meet	Met

	85
O	
LOOK AND LEARN	
OX	
OWL	
ONION	
ORANGE	
OCEAN	

O

MATCH THE WORD WITH THE PICTURE

OX	
OWL	
ONION	
ORANGE	
OCEAN	

O

SPELLING

OX	
OWL	
ONION	
ORANGE	
OCEAN	

O

GRAMMAR

This is an ox.

This is an owl.

This is an onion.

This is an orange.

This is an ocean.

O

SENTENCE

I fed an ox.

I saw an owl.

I ate an onion.

I peeled an orange.

I swam in the ocean.

PRESENT TENSE	PAST TENSE
Feed	Fed
See	Saw
Eat	Ate
Peel	Peeled
Swim	Swam

P

91

LOOK AND LEARN

PAN

POT

PIG

PEN

PUPPY

P

MATCH THE WORD WITH THE PICTURE

PAN	
POT	
PIG	
PEN	
PUPPY	

P	93
SPELLING	
PAN	
POT	
PIG	
PEN	
PUPPY	

P

GRAMMAR

This is a pan.

This is a pot.

This is a pig.

This is a pen.

This is a puppy.

P

95

SENTENCE

I used a pan.

I bought a pot.

I saw a pig.

I wrote with a pen.

I played with a puppy.

P

PRESENT TENSE	PAST TENSE
Use	Used
Buy	Bought
See	Saw
Write	Wrote
Play	Played

Q

LOOK AND LEARN

Queen	
QUILL	
QUILT	
QUESTION	
QUAIL	

Q

	98
MATCH THE WORD WITH THE PICTURE	
QUEEN	
Quill	
QUILT	
QUESTION	
QUAIL	

Q

SPELLING

- QUEEN
- QUILL
- QUILT
- QUESTION
- QUAIL

Q

GRAMMAR

This is a queen.

This is a quill.

This is a quilt.

This is a question.

This is a quail.

Q

SENTENCE

I sang for the queen.

I wrote with a quill.

I have a quilt.

I asked a question.

I played with a quail.

PRESENT TENSE	PAST TENSE
Write	Wrote
Have	Had
Ask	Asked
Play	Played
Sing	Sang

R

LOOK AND LEARN

| RAT |
| RUG |
| ROSE |
| RABBIT |
| RAINBOW |

	104
R	
MATCH THE WORD WITH THE PICTURE	
RAT	
RUG	
ROSE	
RABBIT	
RAINBOW	

R	105
SPELLING	
RAT	
RUG	
ROSE	
RABBIT	
RAINBOW	

R

GRAMMAR

This is a rat

This is a rug.

This is a rose.

This is a rabbit.

This is a rainbow.

R

SENTENCE

I chased a rat.

I sat on a rug.

I bought a rose.

I played with a rabbit.

I saw a rainbow.

PRESENT TENSE	PAST TENSE
Chase	Chased
Sit	Sat
Buy	Bought
Play	Played
See	Saw

S

LOOK AND LEARN

| SUN |
| SKY |
| STAR |
| SNAIL |
| SPOON |

S

MATCH THE WORD WITH THE PICTURE

| SUN |
| SKY |
| STAR |
| SNAIL |
| SPOON |

S

	111
SPELLING	
SUN	
SKY	
STAR	
SNAIL	
SPOON	

S

GRAMMAR

This is the sun.

This is the sky.

This is a star.

This is a snail.

This is a spoon.

S

SENTENCE

I drew the sun.

I looked at the sky.

I saw a star.

I played with a snail.

I bought a spoon.

S

PRESENT TENSE	PAST TENSE
Drew	Draw
Look	Looked
See	Saw
Play	Played
Buy	Bought

T

115

LOOK AND LEARN

TIE	
TEA	
TREE	
TABLE	
TRAIN	

T

MATCH THE WORD WITH THE PICTURE

TIE	
TEA	
TREE	
TABLE	
TRAIN	

T

SPELLING

| TIE |
| TEA |
| TREE |
| TABLE |
| TRAIN |

T

118

GRAMMAR

This is a Tie.	
This is Tea.	
This is a Tree.	
This is a Table.	
This is a Train.	

T

SENTENCE

I wore a tie.

I love tea.

I climbed a tree.

I sat on a table.

I saw a train.

T

PRESENT TENSE	PAST TENSE
Wear	Wore
Love	Loved
Climb	Climbed
Sit	Sat
See	Saw

U

LOOK AND LEARN

UNCLE	
UNIFORM	
UNICORN	
UNICYCLE	
UMBRELLA	

U

MATCH THE WORD WITH THE PICTURE

UNCLE	
UNIFORM	
UNICORN	
UNICYCLE	
UMBRELLA	

U

SPELLING

UNCLE	
UNIFORM	
UNICORN	
UNICYCLE	
UMBRELLA	

U

GRAMMAR

This is my uncle.

This is a uniform.

This is a unicorn.

This is a unicycle.

This is an umbrella.

U

SENTENCE

I love my uncle.

I wear a uniform .

I bought a unicorn.

I rode a unicycle.

I carried an umbrella.

U

PRESENT TENSE	PAST TENSE
Love	Loved
Wear	Wore
Buy	Bought
Ride	Rode
Carry	Carried

V

LOOK AND LEARN

VASE	
VIOLIN	
VEGETABLE	
VOLCANO	
VILLAGE	

V

MATCH THE WORD WITH THE PICTURE

VASE	
VIOLIN	
VEGETABLE	
VOLCANO	
VILLAGE	

V

129

SPELLING	
VASE	
VIOLIN	
VEGETABLE	
VOLCANO	
VILLAGE	

V

130

GRAMMAR

This is a vase.

This is a violin.

This is vegetable.

This is a volcano.

This is a village.

V

131

SENTENCE

I broke a vase.

I I play the violin.

I ate a vegetable.

I saw a volcano.

I visited a village.

V

PRESENT TENSE	PAST TENSE
Break	Broke
Play	Played
Eat	Ate
See	Saw
Visit	Visited

W

LOOK AND LEARN

WELL	
WATER	
Wolf	
WAVE	
WHEEL	

W

MATCH THE WORD WITH THE PICTURE

WELL	
WATER	
WOLF	
WAVE	
WHEEL	

W

135

SPELLING	
WELL	
WATER	
WOLF	
WAVE	
WHEEL	

W

GRAMMAR

This is a well.

This is water.

This is a wolf.

This is a wave.

This is a wheel.

W

SENTENCE

I built a well.

I drank water.

I saw a wolf.

I swam in a wave.

I spun a wheel.

W

PRESENT TENSE	PAST TENSE
Build	Built
Drink	Drank
See	Saw
Swim	Swam
Spin	Spun

X

LOOK AND LEARN

X- FACTOR	
X-RAY	
X-MAS	
XEROX	
XYLOPHANE	

X

MATCH THE WORD WITH THE PICTURE

X FACTOR	
X RAY	
XMAS	
XEROX	
XYLOPHONE	

140

X

	141
SPELLING	
X FACTOR	
X RAY	
X MAS	
XEROX	
XYLOPHANE	

X

GRAMMAR

This is the X Factor.

This is an X Ray.

This is Xmas.

This is a Xerox.

This is a Xylophane.

X

SENTENCE

I went to the X Factor.

I took an X Ray.

I love Xmas.

I copied on a Xerox.

I played the Xylophane.

X

PRESENT TENSE	PAST TENSE
Go	Went
Took	Take
Love	Loved
Copy	Copied
Play	Played

Y

LOOK AND LEARN

YOLK	
YARN	
YACHT	
YO YO	
YAM	

Y

MATCH THE WORD WITH THE PICTURE

| YOLK |
| YARN |
| YACHT |
| YO YO |
| YAM |

Y

SPELLING

YOLK	
YARN	
YACHT	
YO YO	
YAM	

Y

148

GRAMMAR

This is a Yolk.

This is a yarn.

This is a yacht.

This is a yo yo.

This is yam.

Y

SENTENCE

I ate a yolk.

I spun a yarn.

I love a yacht.

I played with a yo yo.

I ate a yam.

Y

PRESENT TENSE	PAST TENSE
Eat	Saw
Spin	Spun
Love	Loved
Play	Played
Eat	Ate

Z

LOOK AND LEARN

ZIP	
ZOO	
ZERO	
ZEBRA	
ZOMBIE	

Z

MATCH THE WORD WITH THE PICTURE

ZIP	
ZOO	
ZERO	
ZEBRA	
ZOMBIE	

Z

SPELLING	
ZIP	
ZOO	
ZERO	
ZEBRA	
ZOMBIE	

Z

GRAMMAR

This is a zip.

This is a zoo.

This is a zero.

This is a zebra.

This is a zombie.

Z

SENTENCE

I bought a zip.

I visited the zoo.

I drink Zero coke.

I played with a zebra.

I look like a Zombie.

Z

PRESENT TENSE	PAST TENSE
Buy	Bought
Visit	Visited
Drink	Drank
Play	Played
Look	Looked

www.ingramcontent.com/pod-product-compliance
Lightning Source LLC
Chambersburg PA
CBHW081348160426
43201CB00014B/2136